Verbs in Action
Carry On

Dana Meachen Rau

Marshall Cavendish
Benchmark
New York

You need a lot of food for the picnic. You use a shopping cart to carry the food in the store.

The clerk puts your food in bags. Now you have to carry all those bags home!

Carry means to bring something from one place to another.

You can carry small objects in your pocket. Pockets are safe places to carry money.

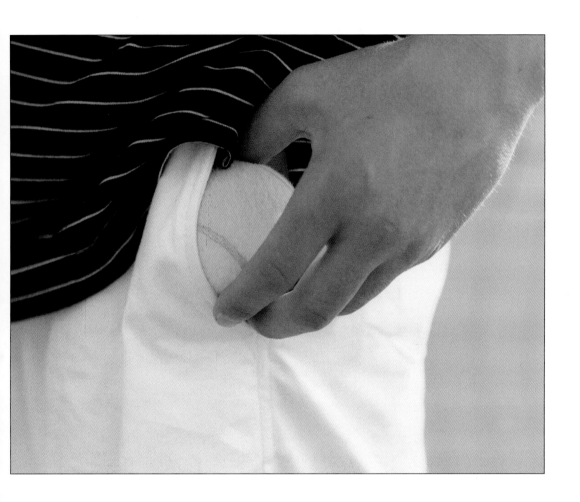

Arms are good for carrying things, too. A mom carries a baby in her arms.

A pile of pillows is easy to carry. Pillows are light.

A chair is a lot heavier. You
might need two people to carry
a chair.

How do you carry your books to school? Instead of carrying them in your arms, you can use your back. A backpack makes carrying books a lot easier.

In some countries, people carry water jugs and baskets on their heads. If they do not have good *balance*, something might fall.

Some objects are much too heavy for people to carry.

How can you carry a pile of rocks? A wheelbarrow is a great way to carry a big *load*.

Trucks carry everything from ice cream to furniture.

People fill the trucks with the *cargo* at a *factory*. Then they bring it to a store.

Elephants can carry heavy logs with their trunks. Birds carry worms in their beaks.

Chipmunks carry seeds in their cheeks.

A koala carries its baby on its back until the baby can live on its own.

Have you ever had a piggyback ride?

Lots of *vehicles* carry people from place to place. A school bus carries children to school.

An airplane can carry you to another country. A hayride carries you through a farm in the fall.

You can "carry a tune" if you have a nice singing voice.

You can get "carried away"
when you cannot stop laughing.

Have you ever complained to your parents? You want to stay up late, but they say no. Your parents might tell you to stop "carrying on" about it.

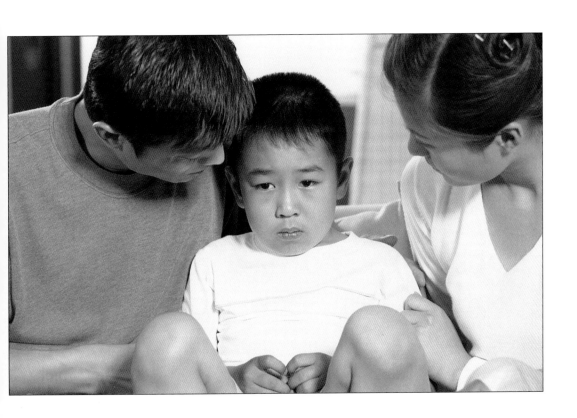

You have a lot to carry on your camping trip. You carry a sleeping bag in your backpack. You carry a bandanna in your pocket. You carry a *compass* around your neck. Now you are ready to go!

Challenge Words

balance (BAL-ents)—The ability to stand straight without falling down.

cargo (KAR-go)—The products a ship or truck carries.

compass (KUM-puhs)—A tool that tells you which direction you are going.

factory (FAK-tuhr-ee)—A place where a product is made.

load—Something that is carried.

vehicles (VEE-i-kuhls)—Machines that bring people from place to place.

Index

Page numbers in **boldface** are illustrations.

With thanks to Nanci Vargus, Ed.D. and Beth Walker Gambro, reading consultants

Marshall Cavendish Benchmark
Marshall Cavendish
99 White Plains Road
Tarrytown, New York 10591-9001
www.marshallcavendish.us

Library of Congress Cataloging-in-Publication Data

Rau, Dana Meachen, 1971-
Carry on / by Dana Meachen Rau.
p. cm. — (Bookworms. Verbs in action)
Summary: "Discusses the action described by a verb, while making connections between people and other living and nonliving objects. It also talks about other uses of the word in commonly used phrases."
—Provided by publisher.
Includes index.
ISBN-13: 978-0-7614-2289-1
ISBN-10: 0-7614-2289-7
1. Carry (The English word)—Juvenile literature. 2. English language—Verb—Juvenile literature. I. Title. II. Series.
PE1317.C37R38 2006
428.1—dc22
2005026785

Photo Research by Anne Burns Images

Cover Photo by SuperStock/RubberBall

The photographs in this book are used with permission and through the courtesy of:
Corbis: pp. 1, 20 Gary Bell/zefa; pp. 3, 22 Tom & Dee Ann McCarthy; p. 5 Gary Houlder; p. 6 A.Inden/zefa; p. 8 Tim Pannell; pp. 9, 11, 15, 29 Royalty Free; p. 12 Keren Su; p. 16 Richard T. Nowitz; p. 18L Enzo & Paolo Ragazzini. ®William Manning; p. 19 Gary W. Carter; p. 21 ROB & SAS; p. 23 W. Deuter/zefa; p. 25 Grace/zefa; p. 27 Yang Liu. SuperStock: pp. 2, 17, 24 age fotostock.

Printed in Malaysia
1 3 5 6 4 2